I'm the
Big Sister Now

I'm the Big Sister Now

Michelle Emmert
illustrated by Gail Owens

Albert Whitman & Company
Morton Grove, Illinois

Dedicated to my sister, Amy,
and all her friends.

Library of Congress Cataloging-in-Publication Data
Emmert, Michelle.
I'm the big sister now / Michelle Emmert; pictures
by Gail Owens.
p. cm.
Summary: Nine-year-old Michelle describes the
joys, loving times, difficulties, and other special
situations involved in living with her older sister
Amy Emmert, who was born severely disabled
with cerebral palsy.
ISBN 0-8075-3458-7 (lib. bdg.)
1. Cerebral palsied children–Juvenile literature.
[1. Cerebral palsy. 2. Physically handicapped.
3. Emmert, Amy.] I. Owens, Gail, ill. II. Title.
RJ496.C4E46   1989   89-5584
618.92'836–dc19   .   CIP
AC

Text copyright © 1989 by Michelle Emmert.
Illustrations copyright © 1989 by Gail Owens.
Published in 1989 by Albert Whitman & Company,
6340 Oakton Street, Morton Grove, Illinois 60053.
Published simultaneously in Canada by
General Publishing, Limited, Toronto.
All rights reserved. No part of this book may
be reproduced or transmitted in any form or by
any means, electronic or mechanical, including
photocopying, recording, or by any information
storage and retrieval system, without permission
in writing from the publisher.
Printed in the United States of America.
10 9 8 7 6 5 4 3 2

Typography by Karen Johnson Campbell.
The text for this book is Lubalin Graph Book.
The illustrations are in pencil and watercolor.

Michelle and Amy Emmert

Amy Emmert, the older sister of the author, was born severely handicapped with cerebral palsy. In this book, Michelle tells her sister Amy's story.

All about Amy

When my sister Amy was born, my mom and dad knew right away that she was going to be a special little girl. Part of her brain did not work because she did not get enough oxygen during birth. This kind of brain damage is called cerebral palsy.

Some people with cerebral palsy have a limp or a hand that is crooked at the wrist so they can't hang onto things. Or maybe they are a little hard to understand when they talk. Some others who can't walk can still run their own wheelchairs. But Amy is severely handicapped. She cannot sit up, use her hands, walk, talk, read, write, or do anything a normal child can do. She has always been in a wheelchair that was made just for her.

Even though she can't do very many things, she is still a great sister, and I would like to tell you about her.

How I Feel about Amy

Amy was five when I was born. I didn't know then that she was different from any other big sister. I liked being near her. She made sounds like me, and I felt happy and safe beside her.

After I grew out of my youth bed, I told my mom and dad that Amy was scared and needed me. But I was the one who was really afraid, so I started sleeping with Amy. When I had a bad dream or was scared of the dark, I just cuddled up to her, and we both went to sleep.

Amy and me cuddling in bed when I was little.

Now I'm not scared of the dark anymore, but I still like to be with Amy. Sometimes I think she is really better than other big sisters. My friends say their older sisters are always bossing them around. Amy never tells me what to do, and she always listens.

Amy gets sick a lot. Once she was so sick we thought she might die. I know she won't live as long as I will, and that makes me sad. I wonder when she will die, and how. I hope it won't hurt her when she dies.

It's lonely at night when Amy is in the hospital, and we are all glad when she comes home. When Amy is well, I don't worry about her.

I don't think I'm jealous of the time Mom and Dad spend with Amy because she can't help being sick. When she's okay, they do special things with me.

As I grow older, I get bigger, like most kids do. But Amy doesn't grow very fast. She is fourteen and looks like she's only five or six. I'm nine, but I can hold Amy or even carry her if I'm very careful. Mom says I've become the big sister because I'm taller and because I help Amy to feel happy and safe. Being her big sister makes me feel good inside, too.

How Others Feel about Amy

One time when I was little, Mom, Amy, and I went to the park. A guy on a huge motorcycle pulled up. He had long, greasy hair and a jacket with the name of a gang on it. My mom was worried he'd cause trouble, and she couldn't see a policeman or anyone else around. But when he got close, Mom saw he had tears in his eyes. He said, "Can I do anything for your little girl?" My mom was relieved and answered all his questions. Amy always brings out the best in people.

When I was about seven, we went to a basketball game. A couple of girls started staring at Amy. I went over to Amy and hugged her. Then I glared at the girls, and they went away. Amy does not like people staring or pointing at her; we think she gets uncomfortable. But we do not mind having people ask questions because it shows they care and are interested. People usually say things like, "Was she born the way she is?" or "Can she walk or talk?" Sometimes they ask whether she's happy or sad when she makes loud noises, or why she always has her mouth open.

I can answer most questions. Her noises are happy or sad depending on what is happening, and she cannot close her mouth completely because of the way it is formed.

Christmas at Grandma's and Grandpa's church.

My family went to my grandma and grandpa's church last year, and someone we didn't know said, "Merry Christmas, Amy." We couldn't figure out how he knew her. But then later we noticed that Amy's wheelchair had a nametag tied on. It made us feel good that people cared enough about Amy to include her.

Sometimes when I go to the pool, Amy will come. She is pretty light and can float without a life jacket if people hold their hands under her head. Little kids five or six years old will float her by keeping her head up out of the water and pulling her around the pool. Sometimes they argue over whose turn it is to float Amy. She laughs a lot while she floats and smiles at the person pulling her. Mom sits right nearby so she can help if Amy starts to slip under.

Amy started going to a special school when she was one year old. All the kids there are handicapped, but in different ways. Some of them can walk a little or play with toys by themselves. Some kids learn to feed themselves and to use the bathroom. The kids who can move their hands but cannot talk learn sign language. With the teachers' help, some kids can paint pictures. There are special exercise mats and balls in the classroom and a "standing board" to help kids stand in front of a desk. Amy likes to play in a big playpen filled with styrofoam.

Teachers from other rooms like to visit Amy, especially when they're sad or lonely. Amy makes people feel happy and important. She is very pretty, and she almost always smiles when you talk to her. Her eyes tell you how much she likes life, and you think, "If she's not sad, then I shouldn't be, because I can do a lot of things." And Amy is a very good listener. You can tell her secrets, and you know she won't tell anyone. She'll listen as long as you want to talk without telling you she's too busy or that what you're saying is stupid. You always feel better after you talk to her.

How to Take Care of Amy

Amy's brain damage was severe, and she cannot even hold her head up by herself. We hold it up for her when we are playing with her, and when she sits in her wheelchair, the high back holds her head up. Her wheelchair also tilts back a little instead of sitting perfectly straight, and that stops her head from falling forward. We push her around the house in the wheelchair and go for long walks outside.

Until she was thirteen, Amy ate regular food, except blended. But when she swallowed her food, she would often choke. Then the food would go down into her lungs instead of into her stomach, and she would get very sick with pneumonia. She would start breathing loudly, and it seemed as if she was working very hard just to push the air in and out. She would also get mucus in her throat, and we had to use a suction machine to get it out. Many times we couldn't make her well at home, and she would have to go into the hospital. Now she has a gastrostomy tube that we feed her through. It is about the size of a pencil and goes straight into her stomach. We get Isocal, a special liquid food, at a drugstore, and she is healthier now than when she ate regular food.

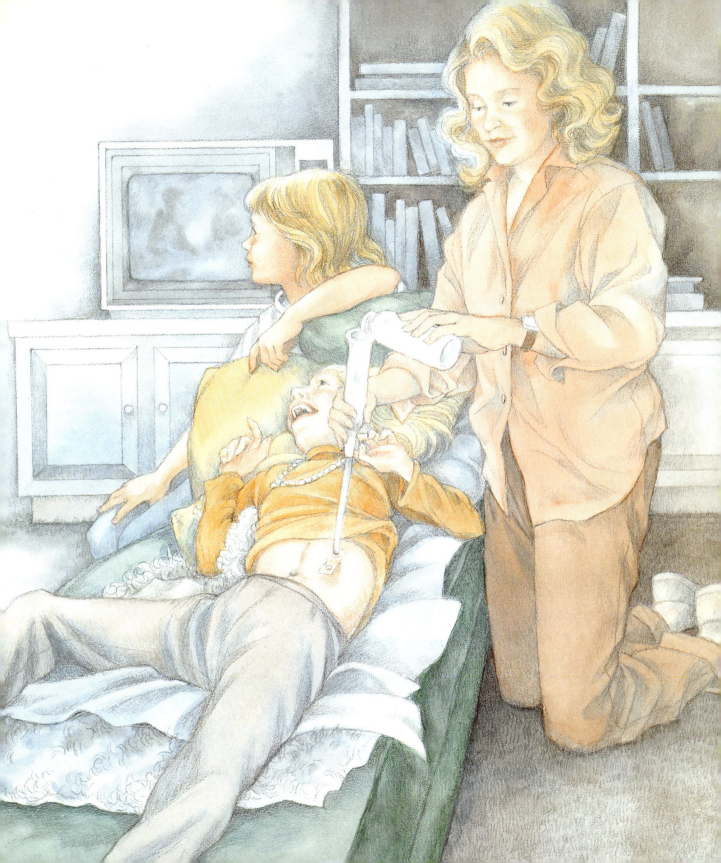

Amy has a special bathtub that my dad and grandpa built in her bedroom. She catches a cold very easily, so when it's time for her bath, we make her room nice and warm. Then we just move her from the bathtub to her dressing table, and we can bundle her up in towels. The tub is higher from the floor than most tubs so whoever bathes Amy will not have to bend too far. It is very shallow because Amy is too heavy to lift out of a deep tub. Dad and Grandpa put a regular toilet under the tub, and we can rinse her diapers right away. Because there is a lot to do to make Amy comfortable, we are trying to make taking care of her easy.

Dad giving Amy a bath.

Amy has a big waterbed in her room. Since she is thin and can't roll over by herself, it would hurt to lie on a regular bed all night. But with her waterbed, she feels like she's floating at the pool, and she doesn't get tired of lying in the same place. A heater in the bed keeps her warm and cozy all the time. My friends and I like to bounce Amy on her bed. We get it rolling like big waves, and she slides back and forth and rolls from side to side. Sometimes she laughs so hard she can hardly get her breath, and we have to stop for a minute. Then we do it again!

If Amy starts crying, I hold her and talk or read to her, and she stops. Sometimes when I babysit Amy, I play with her. If I cough, sneeze, snore, clap, slam drawers, or move my head up and down, Amy laughs. We don't know why she laughs at these weird things, but she does.

Getting ready for Halloween.

Sending Christmas cards.

    Amy likes to watch me do things like play the violin, carve pumpkins, and decorate the Christmas tree. When I send cards to good friends, I help Amy sign the cards with an X or I help her write her name. I put the pen in her fingers, and then I take hold of her hand and move it to make the letters we want. It doesn't look quite as good as if I did it myself, but our friends think it's neat, and so do I. Even though I am younger, I like taking care of Amy.

Special Times in Amy's Life

Before I was born, my dad had a small motorcycle, and he would take Amy for rides. Mom and Dad would strap her to my dad's chest so she couldn't fall off. The pictures look pretty funny, but she loved the rides.

My mom and dad said it was very special for Amy when I was born because she loves babies. She liked it when I learned to crawl by going over her tummy. We used to talk in baby language to each other, too. Amy liked to hold me. She would sit in her wheelchair, and Mom would put me in her lap. Since Amy's arms bend at the elbow and are very stiff, she could hold me without trying. We went everywhere like that until I was about nine months old. Then I became too heavy and squashed her, so I couldn't ride anymore.

Me taking a ride with Amy.

My Grandpa Rupp lives on a farm in Iowa, and when Amy was six, he took her for a ride on his big new tractor. Amy liked being up so high. She laughed a lot.

Until I was about six, we went to Pixieland several times a summer. All the rides were made just for little kids. Amy would pay for one ticket, but she would get as many rides as she wanted on the merry-go-round. The owner of Pixieland liked to watch Amy's eyes open wide and hear her squeal because she was having so much fun on the pretend horses.

Amy swings in something my dad and grandpa invented. It's a chain that we hook up to a regular swing chain. We hook the other end to her wheelchair, and someone pushes her. She can go high enough for my dad to run underneath. She likes it a lot, and when she gets tired, she just stops laughing.

When Amy was nine, she was a ring bearer in our friends' wedding. She wore a long dress with satin ribbons on it. We curled her hair, and she looked beautiful. The night before the wedding, she was so excited that she kept squealing and laughing and making loud sounds. We were worried she would do the same thing during the wedding, but she didn't make a sound until it was all over. We were very proud of her.

Amy's swing.

When Amy has a birthday, she is just like any other person. She is happy, gets presents, and has a birthday cake and ice cream. We used to mash the ice cream and cake for her, but now that she has the gastrostomy tube, she doesn't eat regular food. We always bake her a cake, though, and light the candles when we sing. Birthdays are a fun time for Amy.

Although Amy is loved by a lot of people, I think Mom, Dad, and I are most important to her. We like to do things with her. Last year we got her a bike cart for her birthday. She likes me to pull her in it or in her big wagon. Even on a cold day, Amy and I bundle up, and I take her out. She laughs when we take rides. The bumpier the ride, the better she likes it. When she laughs, she makes me laugh, too.

My sister Amy is a special person. I love her a lot, and I'm glad I told you about her.

People Who Are Extra Special to Amy

Amy has made many friends, but a few have been extra special. These are some.

Aunt Ruthie Schomaker: She is a nurse. She is always there to help when Amy needs something. When Amy was little, Mom used to call Aunt Ruthie in the middle of the night to ask her questions about Amy's temperature or breathing. Amy and I have taken lots of vacations at Aunt Ruthie's house, and we always have the best time.

Colleen Evans' family and Cash, their dog: They all love Amy. Colleen helped take care of Amy for five years. Cash is a St. Bernard with a head the size of a basketball. It is hard for Cash to jump because he is old, but when Amy visits he jumps for her and then lays his head on her lap.

"Uncle" Herbie Rawling: He met Amy when he was in high school, and he cared so much about her that when he got married, he wanted Amy to be a part of his wedding.

Amy and Cash.

Grandpa Rupp with Amy when she was a baby.

Grandpa Rupp: On his visits, he holds, talks, and reads to Amy. When she was a tiny baby and would wake very early in the morning, he would get her up, and the two of them would rock and talk until everyone else woke up. They've been special friends ever since.

Jessie Brees: Because our grandmas and grandpas live far away, Jessie is our "adopted" grandma. She and Amy used to cuddle on the sofa and sing and sing. Amy loves to sing even though she doesn't sound too good. She says, "Ahhhhhhh." Amy and I missed Jessie when she moved.

Vicki Welcome: She was Amy's teacher and took very good care of her. We knew she'd be sure Amy was played with and got moved around when she should and had a sweater on if it got cold. And she used to hug Amy a lot, too.

Mary Ann Smith: Even though she's lived all over the world, she never forgets about Amy. Now she lives nearby and visits Amy often. When Amy was in the hospital, Mary Ann would sit with her and make sure she had everything she needed.

ABOUT CEREBRAL PALSY

Cerebral palsy is the leading handicapping condition in children. It results from damage to the cells of the brain, which have little, if any, potential to recover or replace themselves with new cells. (The number of brain cells you are born with is all you'll ever have.)

This damage causes the various disorders of motion which can range from spastic paralysis of only one arm and leg (*hemiplegia*), to spastic muscles of the lower limbs only (*spastic diplegia*), to severe involvement of all four limbs and trunk (total body involved). Some children have no speech but frequently have the intelligence to understand and to communicate with "inner language." And there are those who are mildly mentally retarded and those, like Amy in this book, who are profoundly retarded. Cerebral palsy is a permanent condition, resulting in a lifelong disability.

Cerebral palsy is most commonly associated with premature birth. Lack of oxygen at birth as a cause is uncommon. In about 25 percent of the children, the cause is unknown but usually thought to result from brain maldevelopment during the very early weeks of pregnancy. Sometimes viruses and chemical disturbances of the body affect the brain cells and result in cerebral palsy.

There is no treatment or therapy to cure the condition. No drugs are really effective except in those children who have an associated convulsive disorder. We prefer to say that cerebral palsy can be "managed" rather than "treated." The management program is goal- or function-oriented so that the person can achieve optimum independence in the activities of daily living, communication, and mobility. Orthopaedic surgery has been successful in preventing serious deformities of the joints which can become painful later in life. In order to reduce the spastic paralysis of the lower limbs, neurosurgeons have recently performed *rhizotomy,* selective cutting of sensory nerve roots which run from the spastic muscles to the spinal cord. Occasionally braces help restrict motion, but they are used sparingly and for a distinct purpose. Fortunately, engineering science and technology have made great strides in providing adaptive equipment to compensate for loss of function in walking and talking.

The major emphasis in the management of the child with cerebral palsy must be on the family, which needs great help and understanding. Without a stable, cohesive, and loving family that accepts the child as a person behind the handicap, and not as an object for pity or "treatment," the goal of optimum independence in a comfortable and happy life cannot be reached. The parents and siblings of the child with cerebral palsy deserve not only our support and admiration but also our gratitude. They and the disabled child tangibly demonstrate the value, dignity, and joy of human life.

Eugene E. Bleck, M.D.
Professor Emeritus of Orthopaedic Medicine
Stanford University School of Medicine